Brain Power

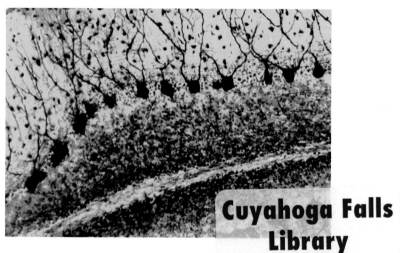

Paul McEvoy and
Sharon Dalgleish

CHELSEA HOUSE
PUBLISHERS
A Haights Cross Communications Company ®

This hard cover edition first published in 2005
by Chelsea House Publishers

CHELSEA HOUSE
P U B L I S H E R S

A Haights Cross Communications ✔ Company ®

Copyright © 2003 Sundance Publishing

Published by
Sundance Publishing
P.O. Box 740
One Beeman Road
Northborough, MA 01532–0740
800-343-8204
www.sundancepub.com

Copyright © text Paul McEnvoy and Sharon Dalgleish
Copyright © illustrations Lloyd Foye and Cliff Watt
Printed and bound in China.

First published 2002 by
Blake Education, Locked Bag 2022, Glebe 2037, Australia
Exclusive United States Distribution: Sundance Publishing

Design by Cliff Watt in association with
Sundance Publishing

Brain Power
ISBN 0-7910-8426-4

Photo Credits:
pp. 6, 10, and 29 photolibrary.com

Table

of Contents

FLIGHT OF THE BALL

WIND DIRECTION

ONE EYE ON THE OPPOSITION

ONE EYE ON THE BALL

SMELL OPPOSITION

HANDS READY TO CATCH THE BALL

RUN FAST

Your Amazing Brain

You see the ball.

You run. You hear the other team closing in.
You feel the wind blow the ball to the left.
You catch the ball!

What helps you run, look, listen, and grab
all at the same time? The answer is . . .
your brain!

What Is a Brain?

Between your ears is a wrinkly, soft, pinkish lump. If you could unzip your skull and take out this lump, it would fit neatly into the palms of your hands. But don't do that! This strange-looking lump is a human brain. And you wouldn't survive without it.

Most other animals have brains, too. The brain keeps check on what's happening in the animal's surroundings. Then it tells the animal's body what to do.

Hey . . . who turned out the lights?

Move our arm, SHAKE THAT LEG!

LEFT SIDE
RIGHT SIDE

Control Center

Cerebrum
Controls thinking, learning, memory, and voluntary movement

Cerebellum
Controls balance and coordination

Brain Stem
The brain's autopilot, which controls functions vital to life, such as breathing and digestion

That's not our job. We're digesting.

Body Helpers in the Stomach

Spinal Cord
A column of nerves that carries signals to and from the brain

Q: What's the best cure for water on the brain?
A: A tap on the head.

Tipping the Scales

Usually, bigger animals have bigger brains. But this doesn't mean they are smarter. They just need a bigger brain to control their bigger muscles and take in information from all that extra skin surface!

SPECIES	AVERAGE BRAIN WEIGHT
sperm whale	7,800 grams (17 lb. 3 oz.)
elephant	6,000 grams (13 lb. 4 oz.)
bottle-nosed dolphin	1,500–1,600 grams (3–3.5 lb.)
human (adult)	1,300–1,400 grams (2.8–3 lb.)
giraffe	680 grams (1.5 lb.)
chimpanzee	420 grams (15 oz.)
lion	240 grams (8.5 oz.)
dog (beagle)	72 grams (2.5 oz.)
stegosaurus	71 grams (2.5 oz.)
cat	30 grams (1 oz.)
rat	2 grams (.07 oz.)

Elephants and whales have the biggest brains. But if you compare brain size to body weight, humans come out on top. A whale's brain makes up about 0.02% of its body weight. Your brain makes up about 2% of your body weight.

My brain is much bigger than a lion's!

I've got a brain the size of a walnut. What's a walnut?

Brain weight = 0.004% of body weight

Yum, yum. I like brains.

ain weight = 0.04% of body weight

Brain weight = 0.1% of body weight

It's the Gray Matter That Matters

The human brain is different from other animals' brains in another way. The thin, outer layer of the brain is much bigger in humans. This part of the brain is called the **cerebral cortex**. In humans, it takes up three-quarters of the total volume of the brain. That's why the human brain is so wrinkly. Those wrinkles are the cortex folding in on itself. It's this large cortex that makes us smart.

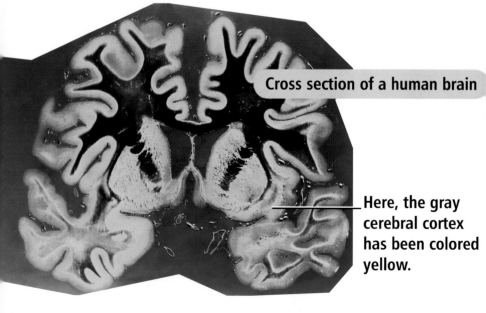

Cross section of a human brain

Here, the gray cerebral cortex has been colored yellow.

Spread out, the human cortex would cover about four sheets of notebook paper.

A chimpanzee's cortex would cover one sheet of notebook paper.

When I'm put in a jar, I turn gray. So would you!

A rat's cortex would just cover a postage stamp.

A fish has almost no cortex at all!

The Two-Sided Brain

The human brain is divided into two halves. The left side of your brain controls the right side of your body. The right side of your brain controls the left side of your body. Why? Because the body's **nerves** cross over at the top of the spinal cord.

Left Brai

Understanding numbers

Speaking

Reading

Solving problems

Are You Left-Brained?

Your left brain puts words together as you talk. It solves problems and is good with numbers.

Many other animals' nerves cross over in the same way. But in a human brain, the two halves of the brain are not **identical**. Each side controls different things.

Right Brain

Painting

Playing music

Judging size, position, and distance

Emotions

Are You Right-Brained?
Your right brain is more creative. When you draw, write, or make music, you use the right brain.

Brain Changes

You were born with your brain already switched on.

Take a new computer out of the box, plug it in, and it starts to work. In contrast, a newborn baby's brain is already working and it is powered by food.

Starting Up

A newborn baby's brain already has a full set of brain cells, called **neurons**. But it is one quarter the size of an adult brain. So why does the brain get bigger as the baby grows up? The answer is in the wiring. A baby's brain might have all the neurons it will ever need, but those neurons are not all connected. The basic parts of a baby's brain are already wired at birth. Those are the parts that control vital things like breathing, sucking, and swallowing.

Q: What were the baby computer's first words?
A: "Da-ta!"

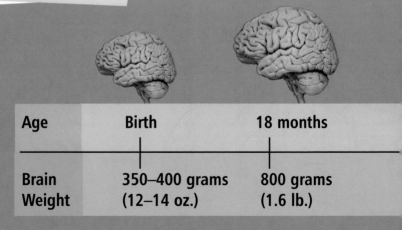

Age	Birth	18 months
Brain Weight	350–400 grams (12–14 oz.)	800 grams (1.6 lb.)

Newborn babies don't fully understand everything going on around them because their brain neurons are not yet connected.

It's a lot of work connecting 100 billion neurons!

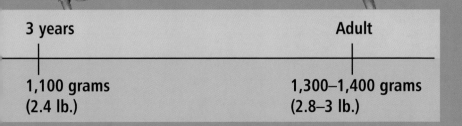

3 years	Adult
1,100 grams (2.4 lb.)	1,300–1,400 grams (2.8–3 lb.)

All Wired Up

The newborn baby's cortex starts out as a mass of unwired cells. It has no memories or experiences to make sense of the world. But it doesn't stay that way for long. Like a computer loading a new program every day, a brain learns quickly.

When developing sight, a baby's brain first tunes in to shapes, colors, and motions.

Once shapes and colors are clear, the baby is ready to notice more complex differences.

Sight, touch, sound, smell, and taste are the brain's first programs. Every experience makes a connection in the human brain. A baby's brain can form as many as two million new connections a second!

YOU DO THE MATH!
You have 100 billion cells in your brain, each connected to as many as 25,000 others. That means 25,000 x 100 billion—which equals 2.5 million billion connections in your brain! So the human brain is far more complex than any computer.

Cross section of the brain, under the microscope

Cell bodies of neurons

Sending Signals

In your brain, electrical signals called nerve signals are passed from neuron to neuron along the **axons** and **dendrites**. It's a bit like the tiny wires that carry electrical signals around the circuits of a computer.

Wiggle your big toe. How did the message get from your brain down to your big toe? The nerve signals were carried down your spinal cord. It connects the rest of your body to your brain. The brain, the senses, the spinal cord, and nerves all work together as the nervous system.

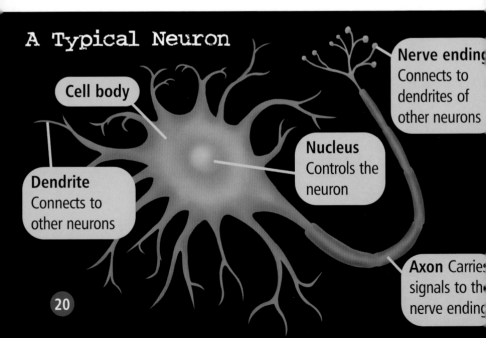

A Typical Neuron

Cell body

Dendrite
Connects to other neurons

Nucleus
Controls the neuron

Nerve ending
Connects to dendrites of other neurons

Axon Carries signals to the nerve ending

The Nervous System

Every second, millions of nerve signals reach the brain from the senses.

Every second, millions of nerve signals go out from the brain.

Spinal cord

A network of nerves branches out to reach the different parts of the body.

Nerve signals can travel faster than 400 km/h (249 mph).

If you laid out all of the body's nerves end to end, they would measure about 75 km (47 miles).

All this high-speed driving makes me nervous!

A Nerve Signal

Use It or Lose It

Your brain never quits!

Even when you rest, your brain keeps working. It makes up only about 2% of your body's weight, but it uses about 20% of your body's energy. So a lot of what you eat is needed to power your brain.

Memory Workout

If you exercise your muscles, they grow in size and strength. It's the same with your brain. When you use your brain, it makes new neuron connections. And as experiences are repeated, those connections are made stronger.

Strong connections lead to strong memories. Memory is the ability of the brain to store and recall information. You have **sensory** memory, short-term memory, and long-term memory. They are all processed and stored in different parts of the brain.

Musicians practice so much that they can play from memory. Some musicians can play up to 1,000 notes per minute, in exactly the right order.

Boost your Brain Power

You can train your brain to remember better! Look at this list for 20 seconds. Then cover it and write down all the things you can remember.

The heat is on!

lemonade
elephants
flour
toothbrush
tonsils
onions
radishes
insects
giraffes
hiccup
toaster

How many items did you remember?

If you remembered everything, your brain is really cooking! Now look at the list again. What phrase do the first letters of each item spell? You can use this phrase, *left to right*, as a memory prompt for each item. Or you can make up a short story using all of the words to help you remember.

Using devices like this when you study for tests can ease the strain on your brain!

Brain Tricks

You can't always believe what you see! Even if you have perfect vision, you can be tricked into seeing things that aren't really there. The brain takes shortcuts. It makes sense of an image by comparing what it sees with what it already knows. This makes the process of seeing much faster. But sometimes the picture doesn't quite match reality. Try these **optical illusions** on your own brain.

Look at these optical illusions and answer the questions.

A

What happens when you stare at this spiral?

Whoaa!

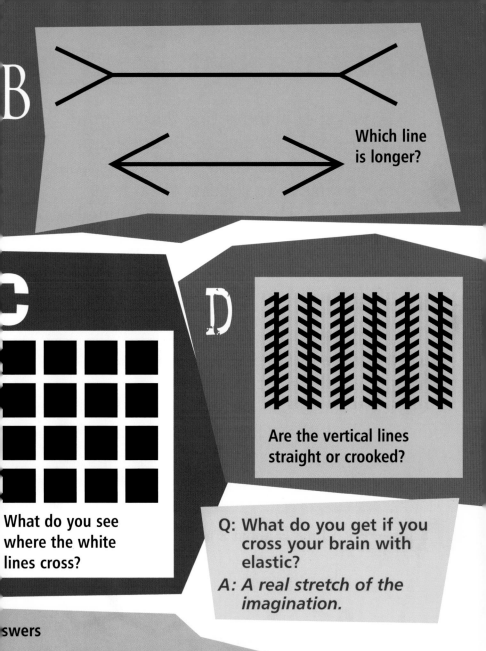

B

Which line is longer?

C

What do you see where the white lines cross?

D

Are the vertical lines straight or crooked?

Q: What do you get if you cross your brain with elastic?

A: A real stretch of the imagination.

swers

A It feels like the spiral is sucking you in.

B Both lines are the same length.

C You see gray spots, but it is really whit

D The vertical lines are straight.

Give It a Rest

You will spend about one third of your life asleep! Sleep gives your body time to rest and repair itself. It also gives your brain a chance to process the day's experiences. This helps you to remember and learn.

Dream On

This graph shows the cycles you go through every night. During the first sleep cycle, brain activity slows down. Then after about 90 minutes, brain activity becomes similar to when you are awake. This is called REM (Rapid Eye Movement) sleep. This is when you dream. REM sleep happens about every 90 minutes throughout the night.

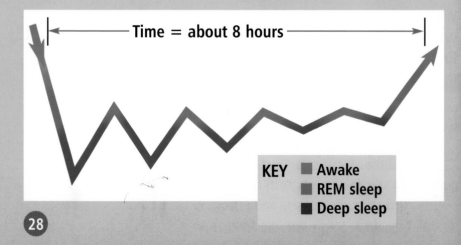

Time = about 8 hours

KEY ■ Awake
■ REM sleep
■ Deep sleep

Red areas show activity

Mmmm . . .
one scoop
or two?

Scientists still have a lot to learn about sleep and the brain. But we've come a long way since the ancient Egyptians. They didn't think the brain was very important. When making a mummy, they would simply scoop out the brain through the nostrils and throw it away.

NOW THAT'S a brain drain!

29

Fact File

The sea squirt is born with a brain. But once it finds a rock, the sea squirt eats its own brain and lives happily ever after.

When a Chicago woman had a brain scan, doctors found out that she had three brains!

That one! That one! That one!

Sorry, you can't make a withdrawal.

The world's largest brain bank is in Belmont, MA. About 350 brains a year are donated to it for research.

The brain can survive for a few seconds without the body. After a man was beheaded in 1905, a doctor called his name three times. And three times the eyes opened and looked at the doctor.

Brain on the loose

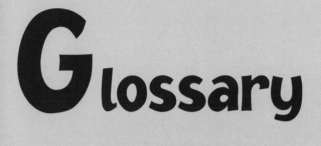Glossary

axons the long "tails" that carry signals away from a neuron

cerebral cortex the wrinkly outer layer of the cerebrum

dendrites the "arms" that carry signals to a neuron

identical exactly the same

neurons cells that make up the brain, spinal cord, and nerves

nerves bundles of neurons that link all body parts to the brain

optical illusions things we see that trick the brain by giving a false impression

sensory to do with the senses—sight, touch, smell, taste, hearing

Index